My First
Odd One Out

Illustrated by Hazel Quintilana & Alex Willmore
Written by Joe Potter
Designed by Anton Poitier & Ben Potter

B.E.S.
PUBLISHING

First edition for North America published
in 2019 by B.E.S. Publishing Co.

Copyright © iSeek Ltd. 2018

All inquiries should be addressed to:
B.E.S. Publishing Co.
250 Wireless Boulevard
Hauppauge, New York 11788
www.bes-publishing.com

This book was conceived, created, and
produced by iSeek Ltd.
RH17 5PA UK

ISBN: 978-1-4380-1271-1

Date of Manufacture: December 2018

Manufactured by: Shenzhen Caimei Printing Co.,
Shenzhen, China

Printed in China

9 8 7 6 5 4 3 2 1

Be different!

This book is jam-packed with odd one out puzzles. Find what's odd and what's not on every page!

Use a pencil, then you can erase it if you get something wrong. If you get stuck, just turn to the back of the book and look at the answers.

There are questions on every page too. Circle the differences and fill in the answers to the questions with a pencil. Have fun!

Circle the duck that is the odd one out.

One duck is u____r the water.

Circle the odd one out in each row.

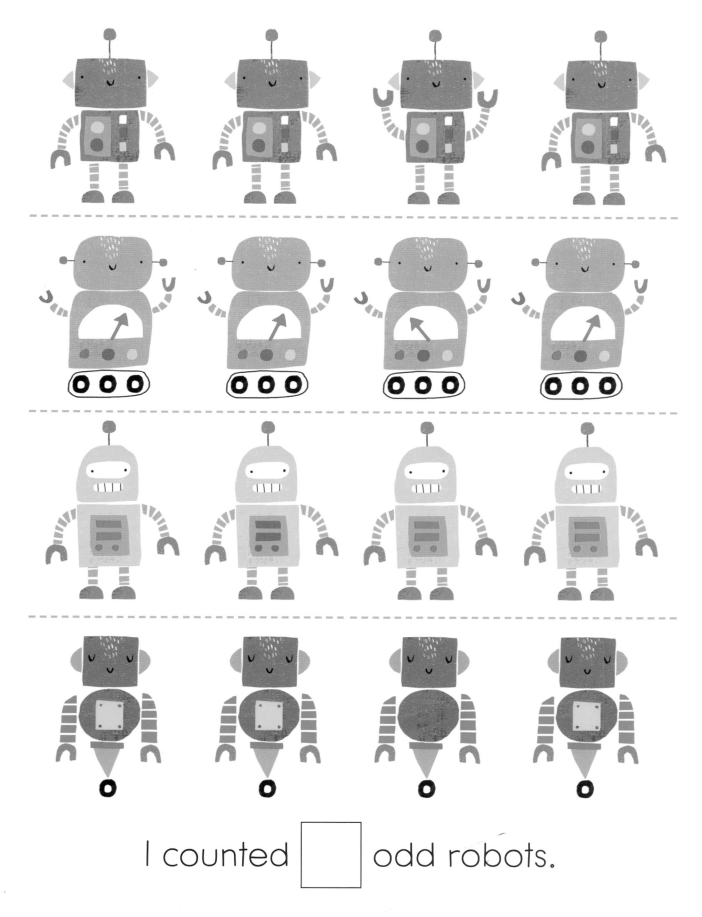

I counted [ ] odd robots.

Who is the odd one out?

The odd one out is a b_y.

Which starfish is the odd one out?

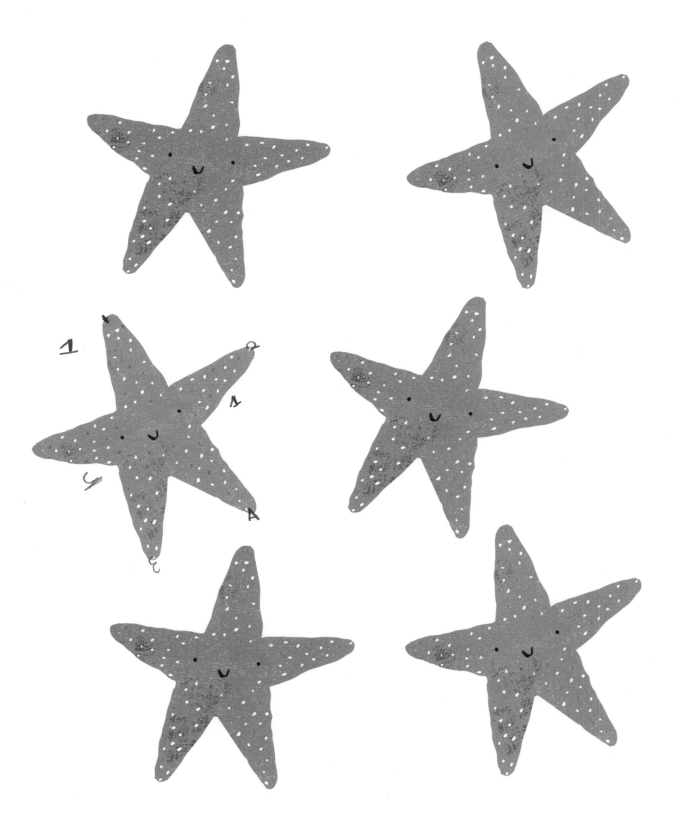

The b____ starfish is the odd one out.

Which pencil is the odd one out?

The blue pencil is upside d__n.

Which tree is the odd one out?

One tree is missing a b_____h.

Which shape doesn't have a pair?

The y_____ shape has no pair.

Why is one sun sad?

The sun is sad because of the c_____s.

Which paint splat doesn't have a pair?

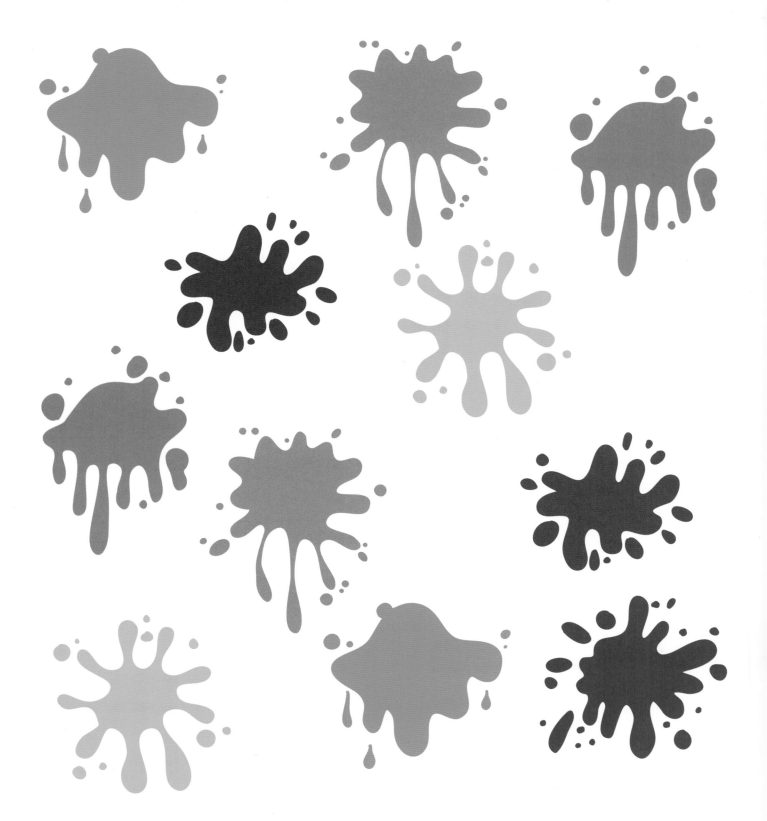

The p_____e paint splat has no pair.

Someone's in a twist! Which one?

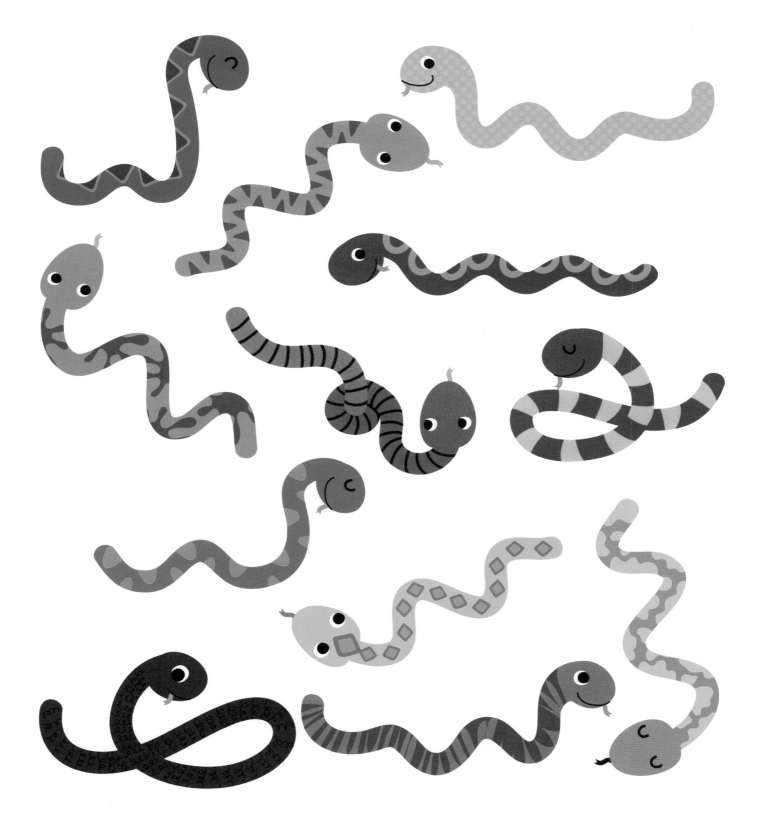

It's the r_d snake with the black stripes.

Circle the footprint that is the odd one out.

It appears to be a b__r footprint.

Circle the pair of daisies that is the odd one out.

I counted ☐ pairs of daisies.

Which fish is the odd one out?

The fish with blue s_____s
is the odd one out.

Which mountain is the odd one out?

One mountain has no s__w.

Circle the coin that is the odd one out.

The odd one out is the [   ] cent coin.

What's odd about the odd one out?

The odd one out is missing a c_____y.

Which playing card has no pair?

The ☐ of hearts has no pair.

Which building is the odd one out?

The c _ _ _ _ e is the odd one out.

Which key doesn't have a pair?

It's one of the y_____w keys.

Which pair are wearing different hats?

The b___s are wearing different hats.

Which sum is the odd one out?

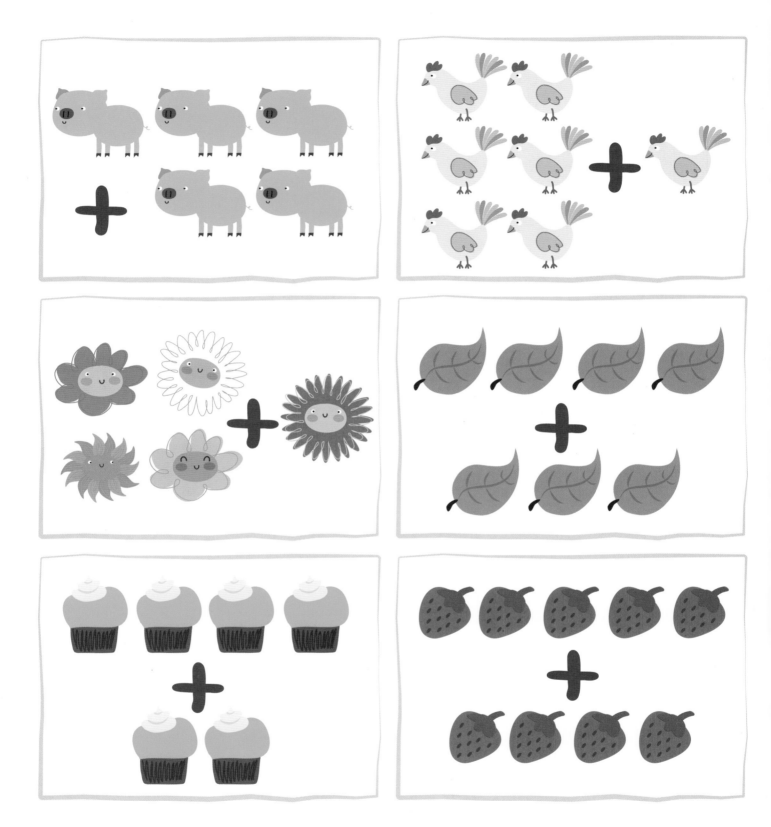

It's the sum with f_____s.

Circle the odd one out in each row.

I found ⬚ odd ones out.

Circle the odd one out in each row.

I found ☐ odd ones out.

Circle the monkey that is the odd one out.

It is the g__y m_____y that is hiding.

Circle the odd one out in each row.

Count the fruits you can see:

Circle the balloon that is the odd one out.

One balloon is flying u_____e down.

Circle the odd one out in each row.

Count the number of red things:

Something on one of these dogs is smaller.

One dog has a short t___l.

Circle the caterpillar that is the odd one out.

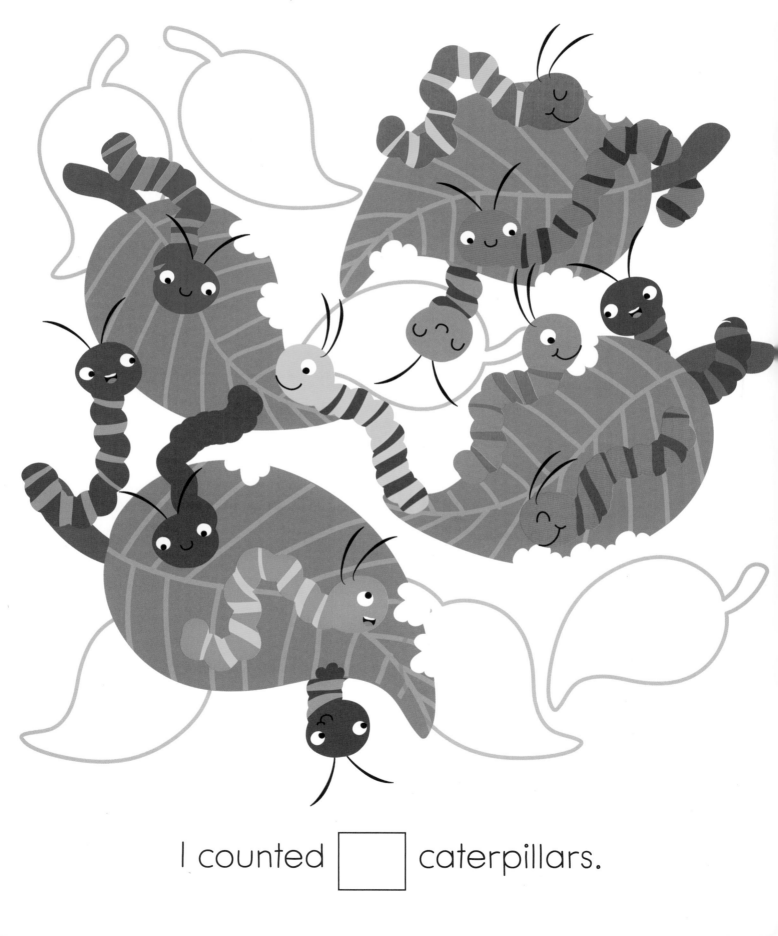

I counted ☐ caterpillars.

Circle the present that is the odd one out.

A box is missing a b_w.

Circle the plane that is the odd one out.

It is the plane that has ⬜ engines.

Which rabbit is the odd one out?

It is the rabbit eating a c_____t.

Which elephant is the odd one out?

It is the elephant going the w___g way.

Which one doesn't have a pair?

The b_ _ _t has no pair.

Circle the pair of flowers that is the odd one out.

One pair doesn't m____h.

What's missing from one of the gingerbread men?

A b_____n is missing.

Which tiger is the odd one out?

One of the tigers has s____s.

Which dancer is the odd one out?

It is the dancer standing on o_e leg.

Which dice doesn't have a pair?

The dice with the number ☐ has no pair.

Circle the cow that is the odd one out.

One cow has big w___e spots.

Circle the whale that is the odd one out.

I counted ☐ whales.

Find the odd ladybug in each row.

I found ☐ odd ladybugs.

Find the odd chick in each row.

I counted ☐ odd chicks.

Circle the owl that is the odd one out.

I counted ☐ owls.

Circle the odd one out in each row.

I found ☐ odd ones out.

Which one of these dinosaurs is different?

It is the one that shows no t___h.

Circle the odd one out in each row.

I found ☐ odd ones out.

Which teddy is the odd one out?

The teddy wearing a b_w tie is the odd one.

Circle the odd one out in each row.

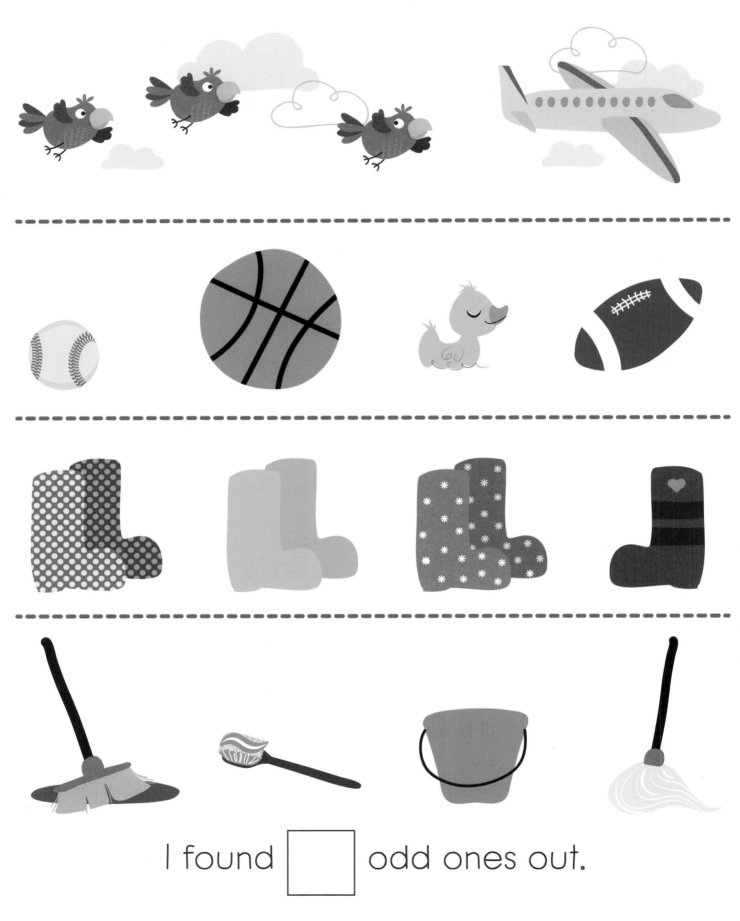

I found ☐ odd ones out.

Which cat is the odd one out?

It is the cat with the empty b__l.

Which bee is the odd one out?

The bee on the f_____r is the odd one.

Which penguin is different?

The penguin with the b__y is different.

Which animal doesn't live on the farm?

The l__n doesn't live here.

Who is the odd one out?

The o_____s is the odd one out.

Which vehicle driver is in the wrong place?

The r___t is in the wrong place.

Which bird is the odd one out?

It is the bird flying in the
opposite d_____n.

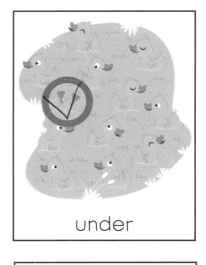

under

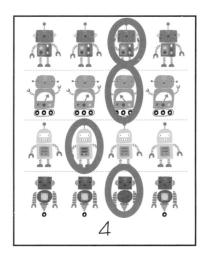

4

boy

blue

down

branch

yellow

clouds

purple

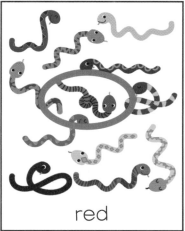

red

bear

13

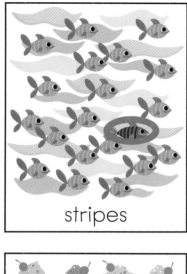

stripes

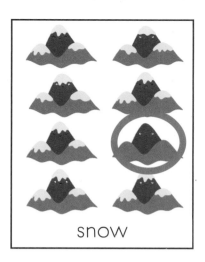

snow

3

cherry

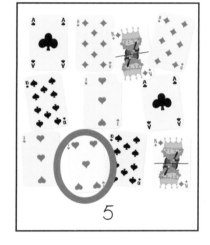

5

castle

yellow

boys

flowers

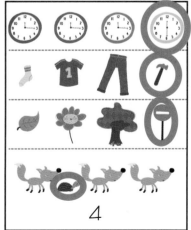

4

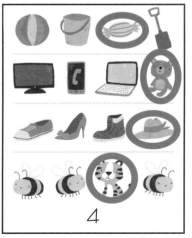

4

gray monkey

3

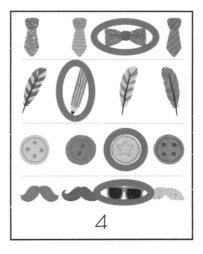

upside

4

tail

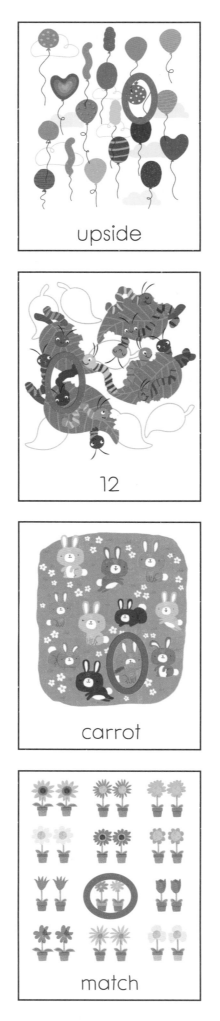

12

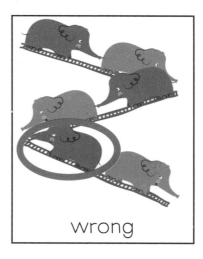

bow

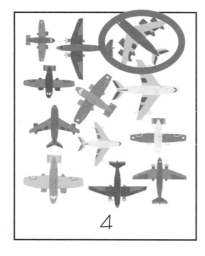

4

carrot

wrong

boat

match

button

spots

one

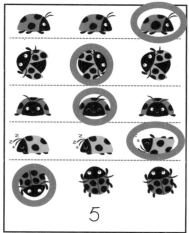

5

white

7

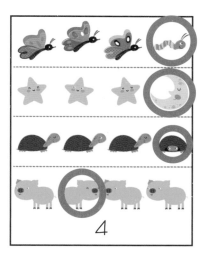

5

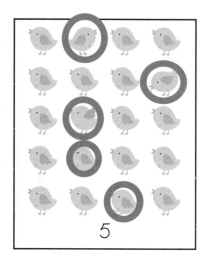

5

12

4

teeth

4

bow

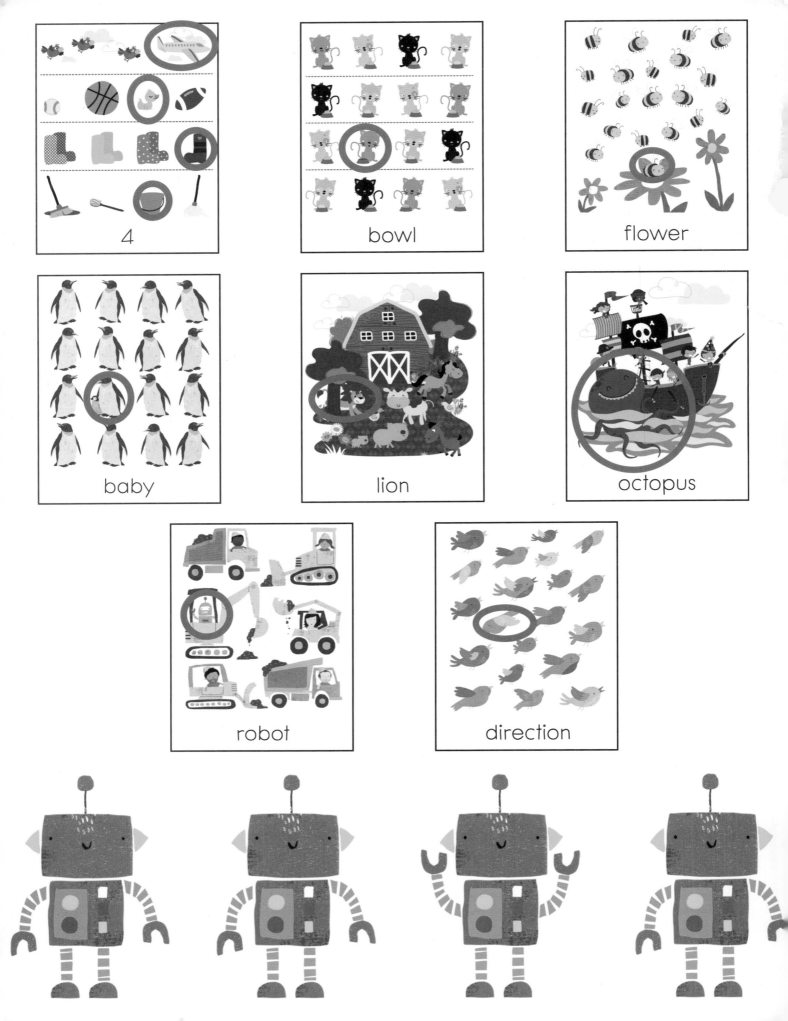

4

bowl

flower

baby

lion

octopus

robot

direction